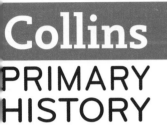

Collins
PRIMARY
HISTORY

C000135822

The Maya
Pupil Book

Alf Wilkinson

William Collins' dream of knowledge for all began with the publication of his first book in 1819.
A self-educated mill worker, he not only enriched millions of lives, but also founded a flourishing publishing house.
Today, staying true to this spirit, Collins books are packed with inspiration, innovation and practical expertise. They
place you at the centre of a world of possibility and give you exactly what you need to explore it.

Collins. Freedom to teach.

Published by Collins
An imprint of HarperCollins*Publishers*
The News Building
1 London Bridge Street
London
SE1 9GF

Browse the complete Collins catalogue at
www.collins.co.uk

Maps © Collins Bartholomew 2019

10 9 8 7 6 5 4 3 2 1

ISBN 978-0-00-831085-1

British Library Cataloguing-in-Publication Data
A catalogue record for this publication is available from the British Library.

Author: Alf Wilkinson
Publisher: Lizzie Catford
Product developer: Natasha Paul
Copyeditor: Sally Clifford
Indexer: Jouve India Private Ltd
Proofreader: Nikky Twyman
Image researcher: Alison Prior
Map designer: Gordon MacGilp
Cover designer and illustrator: Steve Evans
Internal designer: EMC Design
Typesetter: Jouve India Private Ltd
Production controller: Rachel Weaver
Printed and bound by Martins the Printers

MIX
Paper from
responsible sources
FSC™ C007454

This book is produced from independently
certified FSC™ paper to ensure responsible
forest management.

For more information visit:
www.harpercollins.co.uk/green

Contents

It might be difficult to believe, but 200 years ago very few people knew anything about the Maya. There were vague rumours about strange ruins in the jungle, and tales of hidden treasure, but no one really knew anything definite about this mysterious **civilisation**. It was said that the ruins had been built a long time ago by the Ancient Egyptians, **Phoenicians**, Ancient Greeks or even Welsh **explorers**. But they certainly could not have been built by the local tribes!

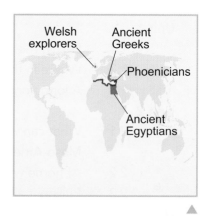

▲ The people Victorians thought built the ruins in the jungle

Finding a ruined civilisation

Two men changed all that. John Stephens (an American businessman) and Frederick Catherwood (an English painter) had both been exploring the ruins of Ancient Egypt when they met in London. They decided to go on an expedition to Central America to explore the ruins there and discover more about the people who built them. Stephens bought a map of the area from a man in New York City, but was told that the map wasn't very accurate! In 1839, they set off from New York on their first expedition. The results were published in 1841 in their book, *Incidents of Travel in Central America, Chiapas, & Yucatán.* Getting there was not easy.

Just to get there took weeks! They had reached the ruins of the Maya city of Copan.

Exploring the ruins

Stephens bought the site of the ruined city of Copan for $50 and began to explore the ruins. When they asked the local Indians who built the ruins, they replied, 'Who knows?' They found ruined buildings, temples, palaces, a ball court and carved sculptures and stairways. When they moved on to another city called Palenque, they set up camp on the floor of a ruined palace! All the time, Stephens was exploring and Catherwood was sketching and painting whatever they discovered. They began to believe that the ruins were from a major civilisation that had developed in the jungle and then died out. After they returned home and published their book, many others followed in their footsteps. Gradually, more and more cities were discovered hidden in the jungle and more and more was discovered about the Maya.

Maya cities are still being discovered today!

Source A: Copan, sketched by Frederick Catherwood in 1839

Think about it!

1. Why do you think people at the time thought the local tribes could not have built the mysterious cities in the jungle?

2. Look carefully at the painting by Frederick Catherwood (Source A). How useful is it to us as evidence of the ruins? How easy would it have been to explore the ruins? How can you tell the place has been abandoned for quite a while?

3. How did the work of Stephens and Catherwood begin to change people's attitudes towards the Maya?

Let's do it!

1. Research the route Stephens and Catherwood would have taken from New York to the jungles of Mexico. What sort of transport would they have used? How easy would the journey have been?

2. What was it like travelling through the jungle? Pretend you are going through the jungle, and write a couple of entries for your diary.

Key words

civilisation
Phoenicians
explorers

If you look closely at the map, you can see clearly just how many modern-day countries were a part of where the Maya lived. Of course, not all these cities were important at the same time, which we will discover. Perhaps you can work out from the map why historians talk about the Maya being '**Meso-American**'.

Major Maya cities and towns

Not just one empire

The Maya were like the Ancient Greeks. They weren't one country or empire, but many separate **city-states**. Each had its own ruler, and the city-states would often fight each other. A strong ruler could make his country bigger, whereas a weak ruler was likely to lose control of his country to a stronger neighbour. So individual city-states grew and shrank over time. They were only as strong as their ruler. However, all the Maya did speak a similar language, although some did find it hard to understand each other!

Clue: 'Meso' comes from the Greek and means 'middle'.

We already know from Unit 1.1 that some of this area is jungle. But did all Maya live in a jungle?

Jungle where the Maya lived

6

Living by the sea

One of the last cities built by the Maya was Tulum. Tulum is on the Caribbean Sea in Mexico and the weather is usually very warm. In Tulum, the hottest month is August, when the average temperature is 32.4 °C. The coldest month is January, when the average is 29.3 °C. There's a dry season and a wet season. In the wet season, there can be up to 464.4 millimetres of rain in a month!

▲ *Tulum*

Think about it!

1. What do you think life would have been like in Tulum?
2. The Maya lived in different small city-states rather than one big country. What difficulties might they experience because of this?

Let's do it!

1. Split into five groups. Research the climate in the rest of Mexico, and in the other countries where the Maya lived (shown in the map). What is the climate like? What's the highest and lowest temperatures? When does it rain? How much rainfall is there each year? You could produce a tourist page for a website or an advert for a newspaper. Present your results to the rest of your group.

2. In what ways is the climate in Tulum similar to the Costa Maya climate? In what ways is it different?

3. What impact do you think the climate of the area would have on the Maya? How might it influence the way they live? Think about how it might affect their houses, their food, their work, and their towns and cities.

Perhaps you have been to Mexico? Costa Maya in Mexico is very popular with tourists from all around the world!

The average temperature in London is 8.1 °C in January and 23 °C in August. Up to 61.6 millimetres of rain can fall in a month!

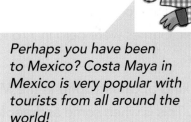

Key words

Meso-American
city-states

The city of Chichen Itza starts in the Northern Lowlands

The Spanish arrive

2000 BCE	1000 BCE	0	1000 CE		2000 CE

First Maya people emerge as farmers in the Pacific coastal areas

Maya begin to build cities

Southern Lowlands cities deserted, 90 per cent of the Maya 'disappear'

The city of Mayapan grows in the Northern Lowlands

Seven million Maya descendants alive

Study the timeline carefully. You will see that the first distinctively Maya settlements date back to around 2000 BCE, and that the Maya start to live in cities around 700 BCE.

What else was happening then?

What other events do you know of that were happening at this time?

The first wheels were used in Mesopotamia around 4000 BCE. The Chinese first made silk around 2700 BCE. Stonehenge was completed by 2000 BCE. Tutankhamun ruled Egypt around 1300 BCE. The Iron Age started in Britain around 800 BCE. The first Olympic Games were held in 776 BCE. Rome was founded in 753 BCE.

Some kind of **catastrophe** in the Maya world occurred around 900 CE. This is when some **archaeologists** suggest 90 per cent of the population simply disappeared. (We will explore this in much more detail in Unit 7.1.) To show how **resilient** the Maya were, a new lot of cities, such as Chichen Itza and Mayapan, were built in the 12th and 13th centuries.

Chichen Itza

What was happening in the rest of the world around 900 CE?

Baghdad was the largest city in the world around 1000 CE, with a population of over 1.5 million, as well as it's famous 'House of Wisdom'. William the Conqueror invaded England in 1066. Christopher Columbus crossed the Atlantic in 1492. This brought the Spanish to Central and South America, and another disaster for the Maya, because the Spanish conquered and destroyed most of the Maya city-states. However, there are still 7 million people of Maya descent alive and well in Central America today.

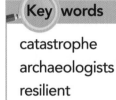

Key words

catastrophe
archaeologists
resilient

Think about it!

1. Study the timeline. When do *you* think is the most interesting time to study the Maya?

Let's do it!

1. Draw a timeline covering the period 4000 BCE to 2000 CE. Carefully add on all the dates you know that relate to the Maya. Don't forget 1839/1840, when Stephens and Catherwood started to explore those mysterious ruins in the Maya jungle!

2. In another colour, add all the non-Maya dates from this page. Next, add any other dates you know from your history lessons.

3. What was the world like when the Maya first started to farm? What was it like when they first built cities? How about when many of them disappeared, around 900 CE? What was it like when the Spanish conquered the Maya, around 1523?

4. Brainstorm a list or a Mind Map of everything you already know about the Maya. Share your ideas with your group or class. Next, think about what you would like to know about the Maya and write a list of questions. Choose your top three questions and then do research to find out the answers.

The Maya today

Estimates vary, but living today in Central America there are around 7–8 million people descended from the Maya, mainly in the areas the Maya have always inhabited. Some live in cities, others in towns, but many still live in the countryside, where they work in farming. Like people all over the world, some are rich and some are poor. One way or another, most still maintain links to their traditional way of life. This can help us to find out about the lives of the Maya who lived long ago.

A visit to the market!

Chichicastenango, in Guatemala, is famous for its traditional market, which is held every Thursday and Sunday. It is the largest traditional market in the whole of Guatemala. People come from far away to buy and sell their produce. Many arrive the evening before the market starts, to set up their stall and even to sleep in the street ready for an early start. About 40 per cent of Guatemala's population are descended from the Maya.

A traditional Maya market

Textiles being sold at a Maya market

Think about it!

1. Imagine you are visiting Chichicastenango market. What can you hear? Smell? See? What is for sale in the market? Who shops there? Who does the selling?

2. Why do you think this market is so important to local people?

3. In what ways is Chichicastenango similar to a market you have visited recently? In what ways is it different?

4. What could we tell about the lives of the Maya from a visit to Chichicastenango market? What can we learn about their clothes, their food and the things they make?

Clothes

The Maya are well known for their brightly coloured textiles. They are woven into capes, shirts, blouses and dresses, and often made of cotton. Each village has its own distinctive pattern, which makes it easy to tell where a person comes from. Women wear a shirt and a long skirt. However, as you can tell from the photographs of the market, many people (especially the men and boys) now wear modern casual clothes.

At home with the modern-day Maya

Some Maya still live in traditional-style houses, like this one in a village in Costa Maya. Look carefully at the photograph, and try to work out what the house is made from.

In the garden

In the gardens surrounding their houses, Maya women grow tomatoes, vegetables, peppers and fruits, as well as flowers to sell in the nearby market. They keep animals, including chickens and turkeys for eggs and meat, and maybe some bees for honey. They hunt wild animals for food. They grow corn, squash and beans in fields nearby. The fields are sometimes still cleared using the traditional '**slash and burn**' technique. Hillsides are often terraced, which provides more land for growing crops.

A traditional Maya house

Wood for new houses is still cut during the full moon. This makes sure it will not be damaged by wood-boring insects!

Traditionally, men worked in the fields too. Nowadays, many men go away to work on **plantations** that grow food and cotton for export, or they work in the tourist industry. Most villages have schools for the children. And it is quite common to see an adult using a digging stick right next to a teenager using a mobile phone!

Cooking tortillas

Eating

Most meals use maize. This is either cooked on the cob or in stews with meat, or in tortillas cooked from maize flour. To make this, the maize must be soaked in water and lime overnight. Then it is ground, using a *metate*,

or grinding stone, to turn it into flour. The flour is mixed with water to make a paste, rolled out flat and cooked into tortillas. Traditionally, the women would use a pottery slab, but today this is more likely to be a metal pan or tray. Tortillas are not just bread, but act also as knife and fork. They are often stuffed with meat or vegetable stews.

A woman using the traditional belt loom

Crafts and earning money

Many women still use the traditional belt loom, like this one, to produce textiles – for their own use and (as we have seen) to sell in the markets. What do you think are the advantages and disadvantages of using such a loom? Other Maya produce traditional-style pottery and wooden carved masks, either to use in the home or to sell.

Key words

'slash and burn'   plantations

Think about it!

1. Look at the photograph of a traditional house. Why do you think the Maya built their houses on small platforms?

2. What would it be like to live in a traditional Maya house? How similar, and how different, would it be to your own home?

3. How self-sufficient are many of the Maya today? What do you think they need to buy? What do they make for themselves? What do they make to sell?

Let's do it!

1. Find out how many different types of maize the Maya grow.
2. Research 'slash and burn' agriculture.
3. Find out all the foods the Maya gave us. The list will include tomatoes and chillies. Try to imagine what your diet would be like without Meso-American foods.
4. If you could meet a modern-day Maya, what questions would you like to ask them?

Tourism

In Mexico, the Costa Maya has become a major holiday destination for visitors throughout the year. For example, in 1970, the biggest resort, Cancún, had a population of three. By 2014, it had 700,000 residents, with 3.5 million tourists visiting each year. People flock to the beach, enjoying the sun, sea and sand. Some also go to visit the ruins of Maya cities and towns. Many Maya have found work as waiters, chambermaids and cleaners. This work is often part-time or **seasonal**, and usually low-paid. In the 'off season', people return to their villages and live with their families.

Let's do it!

1. Research the tourist industry in the Costa Maya. What are the key attractions of the area? Which is the best time of year to visit? Present your findings to the rest of your class.
2. How has the tourist industry been good for the Maya?
3. Have there been any negative impacts?
4. Finally, compare the impact tourism has had on the Maya around Chichicastenango in Guatemala and around Cancún. How are they similar, and how are they different? What might be the impact of tourism on the way the Maya live today?

Continuity and change

One of the most important skills in studying history is continuity and change. We need to think about *how* things have changed and *how* they have stayed the same. Studying the modern-day Maya gives us an opportunity to see how some things have changed, and other things have stayed the same.

Most things in history do not just happen by chance, but for a reason. Therefore, we also need to think about *why* things change.

We can learn lots about the life of the Maya long ago from the way many Maya still live today.

Think about it!

1. Many tourists go to the markets to buy traditional Maya goods to take home with them as a souvenir. How might this affect the kind of things Maya people make to sell in the market? How can we be sure that what we learn about the Maya today is similar to the Maya of long ago?

2. This unit has looked at how some of the Maya live today, often in a way that is quite traditional. Look back over Units 2.1 and 2.2. Make a list of all the aspects of Maya life you have discovered.

Draw up a table with two columns, like this:

Traditional way of life	Modern way of life

Using *only* the items in the 'Traditional way of life' column, write a short account describing how the Maya live today.

Think about the Maya 1000 or 2000 years ago. Go back to the Mind Map you made in Unit 1.3, and the list of questions about the Maya you had. Has your work in Unit 2 answered any of these questions, or has it created more unsolved puzzles?

What have we learned from the Maya alive today about the way of life of the Maya of long ago?

Key word

seasonal

Geographers split the Maya world into three main areas. The Highlands, or Southern Uplands, is mostly forest. The Southern Lowlands are mostly tropical rainforest, and the Northern Lowlands become drier and less forested as you move north. This area is largely limestone. As this is the Tropics, temperatures rarely fall below 20 °C. The wet season is from May to October. The dry season, from November to May, gets hotter and hotter as the rains approach.

The Maya Realm

Gulf of Mexico

Chichén Itzá

Northern Lowlands

Palenque

Southern Lowlands

Tikal

Caribbean Sea

Highlands

Copán

Pacific Ocean

The Maya realm

Living in the rain forest

The Maya used stone axes to cut down trees and make fields. The **brash** was burned. Ash from the volcanoes and the burning brash makes good soil, so the land is quite fertile for a few years, until the **nutrients** are worn out. Then the trees are left to grow again.

> The wet season brings up to 4000 millimetres of rain every year.

The dense **canopy** of the rainforest might be 65 metres high. The forest provided the Maya with many resources. Timber was one of the most important. Sapodilla trees, for example, are very soft when first cut down and ideal for working with. However, once they dry out, they become very hard, which is ideal for buildings or tools. Creepers were harvested and turned into fibre for rope and twine. Honey could be collected (from bees that do not sting), along with other fruit, and rubber, which is used to make the ball for their famous ball game (see Unit 4.2).

Hunting for food

Much of the meat eaten by the Maya was hunted in the rainforest: wild turkeys, small deer, quail, duck, monkeys, iguanas and pacas. The Maya would use a long blowpipe to shoot darts at animals in the tree cover, and use spears and (later) bows and arrows for hunting. They hunted crocodiles in the coastal rivers and swamps, and caught fish – especially shellfish – from the sea.

▲
Rainforest

Water

Despite having lots of rain for much of the year, water was a big problem for the Maya. This was especially the case in the Northern Lowlands, where water drained quickly through the limestone into underground streams and caverns. They had to develop a way to store water for the dry season, so they could water their crops. They used *cenotes*, natural sinkholes, to make sure they had water throughout the year.

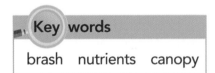

Key words

brash   nutrients   canopy

Think about it!

1. What challenges did living in a rainforest cause the Maya?
2. How did they deal with those challenges?

Let's do it!

1. Draw up a calendar for a whole year, from January to December. For each month, decide what a Maya family might be doing. Use the information you have discovered in Units 2 and 3.1 to complete your calendar.

2. From what you have discovered so far, when was the *best* time of year to be a Maya? When was the *worst*?

3. Research the Maya and the rainforest. How carefully did they look after the resources in the rainforest? In your opinion, were they environmentally friendly?

4. Make a presentation to give to the rest of your class with the title 'The Maya and the rainforest'.

Chocolate!

Cacao pods ripening on a tree

For the Maya, one of the most important trees found in the rainforest was the cacao tree. Originally, this was only found in the Meso-American rainforest. We know it as the source of chocolate.

The cacao tree needed lots of heat and moisture to grow, but it also needed shade. Therefore, it grew perfectly in the forest, sheltered beneath the canopy of taller trees. It grew up to 10 metres tall. The cacao pods were harvested at the end of the rainy season. Each pod contained between 30 and 40 beans, and these were laid out to dry. Once dry, they were crushed into a paste that was added to water and made into a drink. The chocolate was poured from one container to another before it was served, to make it frothy. If you did this in front of your guests, it was a way of showing them how important they were.

As the Maya had no sugar, they flavoured their drink with chillies, vanilla, fruit and flowers.

Chocolate was a very important part of Maya religious life, as well as a refreshing drink. The dried beans were also used as money – they were valuable and easily transported from place to place. A Maya farmer would look after his cacao trees very carefully indeed!

▲
Cacao beans

How Kukulkan gave the Maya chocolate

The Maya told many stories to explain where things came from, or why things happened. Here is an example:

'Kukulkan was one of the Maya gods. Kukulkan and the other Maya gods helped the Maya to grow many crops, with the exception of chocolate – that was reserved especially for the gods. One day Kukulkan was particularly happy, and wanted to give the Maya the gift of chocolate. The gods were angry – they made Kukulkan promise that he would never do such a thing. One night, Kukulkan decided he just had to steal a cacao tree and give it to the Maya. He would plant it, and show the Maya how to grow cacao, how to harvest the pods, how to dry them and then how to turn the dried pods into the gods' favourite drink. So that is what he did. He stole a small cacao tree and gave it to the Maya. He showed them everything they needed to know to be able to grow and harvest the beans and turn them into chocolate. He even showed them how to make chocolate, carefully pouring it from one cup to another until it was nice and frothy – just right to drink. And so that is the story of how the Maya came to love chocolate.'

Thinking about significance

One of the most important skills in studying history is to think about significance – how important someone or something is. This could be importance at the time or it could be how people feel about that person or thing now. For example, someone or something can be significant to us now, but may not have been thought of as important at the time. Unit 3.3 is going to ask you to consider how significant the rainforest was to the Maya.

Significance – how important something or someone was, both at the time and since.

Think about someone who is significant in your own life. Who might that be? Why are they so important in your life? Have they always been that important, or has their significance changed over time? Discussing this will help you to work out exactly what 'significance' means. It will also help you to decide just how significant the rainforest was to the Maya.

Chicle

Chicle (*tsicte* in the Maya language) was a sticky sap that was collected from some trees in the rainforest, much like rubber latex is still collected today. It was allowed to set and became very sticky. Because it was sweet, it was sometimes used in cooking.

A wild turkey
▼

Mainly it was mostly chewed, used as a breath-freshener, tooth-cleaner and to stop people feeling hungry. Until the 1950s, it was widely used throughout the world to make chewing gum!

Deciding if something is/was significant

Ian Dawson, a well-known historian and history teacher, uses these **criteria** for deciding significance. Perhaps you can think of your own reasons why something may or may not be significant.

Something is significant if it:

- changed events at the time
- improved lots of people's lives – or made them worse
- changed people's ideas
- had a long-lasting impact on the country or the world
- had been a really good or a very bad example to other people on how to live or behave.

Think about it!

1. Think about what you have learned in Units 3.1 and 3.2 about the Maya and the rainforest. What did the Maya use the rainforest for? What did it supply them with? Do you think the Maya could have lived the way they did without the rainforest?
2. Why were the Maya careful about how they used the rainforest?

Let's do it!

1. Which do you think was more important to the Maya way of life – farming or exploiting the rainforest? Why?
2. Hold a class discussion about the significance of the rainforest to the Maya. How much did it improve lots of people's lives? How much did it have a long-lasting impact on the country or the world?
3. Finally, do you agree with Ian Dawson's criteria for deciding if something is significant? Or have you developed your own, improved version?

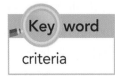

Key word

criteria

The remains of the Royal Palace at Palenque
▼

The Maya lived in up to 50 separate city-states. Not all Maya cities were important at the same time, however. El Mirador, for instance, was important around the year 0; Tikal grew around 600 CE, but was deserted by 900 CE; and Chichen Itza and Mayapan were at their peak later.

Pyramids, palaces and plazas

Some Maya cities were huge. Tikal was home to around 60,000 people. El Mirador covered 26 square kilometres. However, according to Alex Woolf, in his book *The Mayans*, they were all built in the same way. At their heart was a huge plaza or square. This served as a meeting place for ceremonies and festivals, as well as a marketplace. The plaza was dominated by royal palaces, pyramids, **observatories** and temples, as well as houses of the rich and powerful. The less important someone was, the further away from the plaza they lived. People from far away would bring in their taxes – either food or other goods – as **tribute** to the King. He in return, was expected to protect them from danger. The King and his nobles were much better fed and clothed – and much better looked after – than everyone else! The King was also the chief priest. He would decide when to sow crops, when to harvest them

Stela from the city of Copan

and when to hold festivals. He would look very impressive dressed in a robe made from jaguar skins, wearing a headdress of quetzal feathers.

Archaeologists have explored many of these cities to try to understand city life. The palaces and temples were made of stone covered in a kind of plaster, and were decorated with paintings and carvings. The largest buildings were the pyramids. These would usually have a small platform on the top for religious ceremonies. Buildings were frequently built on top of previous buildings or their foundations, which gradually raised them off the ground.

Stelae

Kings liked to brag about their achievements. Therefore, nearly every city, until around 900 CE, has stelae (singular: stela), like this one from the city of Copan. These are free-standing statues that have images of the King on one side and descriptions of his major achievements on the other sides. They were usually put up after a major victory in war.

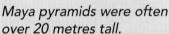

Maya pyramids were often over 20 metres tall.

Key words

observatories   tribute

Think about it!

1. How have archaeologists helped us to understand what it was like living in a Maya city?

2. Why might stelae be important to us when finding out about life in Maya times?

Let's do it!

1. Find out about the jaguar and the quetzal bird. Why could only kings wear quetzal feathers?

2. Split into groups and research different Maya cities. Report back to the class. Then decide whether or not you agree with Alex Woolf that all Maya cities were built in the same way.

3. Imagine visiting the city and arriving in the plaza. What would you see? Smell? Hear? How would you feel? Write a brief account of your visit.

Maya cities were often fighting each other. Their power and wealth expanded or contracted from time to time. It all depended on how strong the King was. Not only was the King expected to be a ruler and religious leader – he was expected to lead his army in war against other cities.

Lady K'abel

We know the names of very few women from Maya times. Lady K'abel is one of them. She was the military ruler of El Peru-Waka between 672 CE and 692 CE. Her tomb was discovered in 2012. Her body was buried with various offerings, including **ceramic** vessels, jade jewellery, stone figurines, and a small **alabaster** jar carved in the shape of a conch shell. Her burial possessions indicate that she was a very important person. She was known as Kaloomte, which translates as 'Supreme Warrior' – higher in authority than her husband, the King.

A drawing of a Maya warrior

Think about it!

1. Why do you think we know so little about the role of women in Maya society?
2. Look carefully at the Maya warrior. What does he wear to protect him from his enemies? What weapons does he have? What would it be like to fight against him?

The ball game

Every Maya city had its own ball court, where teams would play a kind of football. The object was to get the solid rubber ball through a small hoop fixed on a wall of the court. Hundreds of people would watch each game.

Historians disagree about the ball game – the rules, who played it, and what happened to the winners and the losers. Some say each side was made up of high-class captives, who were forced to play, and that the losers were sacrificed to the gods. Others claim that the winners were sacrificed! Some historians think that only nobles and warriors took part. Others suggest it was an **obsession** with the Maya, and everybody – young and old, rich and poor – played it at every opportunity.

The remains of a Maya ball court

Historical interpretation

This is a perfect example of historical interpretation. Historians use the evidence they find and try to explain things – in this case, the ball game. They select the evidence they want to use and then try to reach a conclusion. Of course, the conclusion they reach will depend on which evidence they use! And, if the evidence is **contradictory**, how do you decide what is the 'best' evidence to use? In this case, there is plenty of evidence for historians to use – archaeological, written, even modern-day re-enactments.

Players in the Maya ball game were not allowed to use their hands and feet!

Let's do it!

1. Research the Maya ball game on the internet. What do you think the rules were? How do you think the game was played? Present your findings to the rest of your class. Do they agree with you? Are their conclusions the same as yours?
2. If people in your class think the ball game was played differently to you, can you explain why this is?

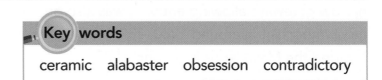

Key words

ceramic   alabaster   obsession   contradictory

Sacrifice!

Sacrifices were a big part of Maya religious ceremonies. Animals, or sometimes humans were offered to the gods in order to arrange a good harvest or a successful war. Otherwise, the King or nobles would cut themselves and offer their own blood as a sacrifice to keep the gods happy.

▲ *The temple of Kukulkan*

The temple of Kukulkan at Chichen Itza

We can learn a lot about Maya cities and beliefs from the temple at Chichen Itza, at the centre of the city. It is a stepped pyramid, 24 metres high, with 91 steps on each side, plus one step to the top (365 steps in total). The temple is positioned so that at the spring and autumn equinox a shadow resembling a snake appears to slither down the steps. Kukulkan is drawn as a serpent god by the Maya. Is this an accident, or is the temple deliberately designed in this way? It does show how clever the Maya were!

The Maya city of Tulum

You may remember from Unit 4.1 that Alex Woolf suggested all Maya cities were built in the same way. Look closely at the ruins of Tulum. Are they the same as any other Maya city you have studied? Tulum was built next to the sea, as a port. It is one of the smallest Maya cities, with an estimated population of only about 1500. It even had a small **beacon** or lighthouse to guide shipping into the harbour. It was surrounded by a wall – 7 metres thick, 5–7 metres high, and nearly 800 metres long – with only five narrow gateways allowing entry. It was also one of the last cities to be built, and was most important in around 1200–1300. It even survived for a while after the Spanish invaded the Maya lands in around 1520.

Tulum was an important trading post. Goods arrived both by land and by sea. **Artefacts** have been found there from the whole of Mexico and all of Central

The Maya city of Tulum

America – evidence of a thriving port. Today, the beach is protected as a breeding ground for turtles. However, Tulum, because it is so close to the Costa Maya, is a major tourist site, and has thousands of visitors every day.

*The Maya used seagoing **canoes** to trade up and down the Caribbean coastline.*

Think about it!

1. Why do you think Tulum was enclosed by such a big wall? What does that tell us about life in the area in the 13th and 14th centuries?

2. In what ways was Tulum similar to other Maya cities? In what ways was it different?

Key words

beacon

artefacts

canoes

Let's do it!

1. Do you agree with Alex Woolf that all Maya cities were built in the same way? Draw up a list of all the evidence you have that supports his view, and a list of all the evidence you have that disagrees with it.

2. Make a short PowerPoint, or poster or other presentation that sums up your arguments.

A modern drawing of a Maya canoe on a river

Roads

The Maya built a huge network of roads. They were known as *sacbeob* (singular: *sacbe*), which translates as 'white roads'. They were built of stone. They were up to 8 metres wide, and raised off the floor of the jungle by about 50 centimetres, to keep them dry. There even appears to be evidence of huts alongside the *sacbeob*, to give accommodation and food at overnight stops.

These roads were used to connect the countryside to the cities. It is said that they held the Maya world together. They also supported a thriving trade network.

The Maya had no animals to pull carts, or wheels, so most items had to be carried by men.

Trade

Life in the big Maya cities depended on trade. Food had to be brought in from the countryside to feed the people in the towns (50,000 people need a lot of food every day!). Some everyday goods like salt were only found in a few places, and rare goods for the King and nobles were often traded over very long distances. Wherever possible, the Maya used canoes on rivers or the sea to transport goods.

Salt

Salt was made from the sea, mostly on the Caribbean coast of Yucatán (see map on page 6). The water was evaporated, then the salt that was left was cut into blocks and traded inland. Everybody needed salt for cooking, but they also used it to preserve meat. Other low-value goods that were traded were fish, and flint and obsidian for tools. Timber, ceramic pots and cloth were also traded over long distances.

Luxury goods

The Maya were a Stone Age people. They had little or no metal, so flint was important for making tools. Obsidian, a glass-like material, was used to make weapons and blades, and was only found in a few volcanoes in the Pacific mountains. Jade was used for jewellery, and again was only found in one or two places. Copper tools and gold pieces were transported from elsewhere in Mexico, and seashells from the Pacific Coast were traded throughout the Maya world. So if your land included a salt factory, or a source of jade or obsidian, then you were very powerful indeed.

Money

The Maya had no money or currency in the sense we know it. Most of their trade was by **barter**, or swapping. Sometimes cacao beans were used as currency, because they were small, they didn't wear out and were easy to transport over long distances. And, if all else failed, you could always drink them!

Key word

barter

Think about it!

1. Why did the Maya go to the trouble of building so many roads?
2. Why was salt so important to the Maya?
3. What would your life be like if we had no money – like the Maya?

Let's do it!

1. Find out where the Maya got hold of obsidian and jade. How were they mined? What were they used for?
2. Can you find out what the Maya exported (sold) to others so they could import (buy) the luxury goods the rulers wanted?
3. Were the Maya rich?

We have already seen that there was a close link between town and the countryside for the Maya. Cities could not exist without farming communities nearby. Also, farmers would only keep supplying the city with food and resources as long as the King kept them safe and secure. But what do we know of the lives of ordinary Maya at the time?

Think about it!

1. Why is it so much harder to find out about the lives of ordinary people so long ago, than it is to find out about the lives of the rich and powerful?

The 'Pompeii of Meso-America'

Ceren is in the country of El Salvador. It is the remains of a farming village that originally dates from around 1200 BCE. It was covered in a thick layer of ash, left over a volcanic eruption around 600 CE. Unlike Pompeii in Italy, the inhabitants of Ceren had plenty of warning, so they were able to escape. Therefore, no bodies have been found in the ruins. Ceren was discovered by accident in 1976, when a bulldozer exposed the remains of a Maya house. Archaeological work started there in 1989. Since then, more buildings have been carefully uncovered. What has been found is staggering. Bed mats, gardening tools, pots still full of beans, furniture, fireplaces and hearths are still largely complete and in place. It is like a time capsule showing what life was like for ordinary Maya around 600 CE.

In 1993, Ceren was made a **UNESCO** World Heritage Site. It is now one of the top tourist destinations in El Salvador.

Remains at Ceren

Is there a UNESCO World Heritage Site near where you live?

More remains at Ceren

Think about it!

1. Look carefully at the images of Ceren. Can you work out what they show? Can you decide how ordinary Maya lived from the sources? What else do you need to know to come to a conclusion?

2. Do you think Ceren should have been added to the UNESCO list? Why?

UNESCO World Heritage Sites

There are over 1000 UNESCO World Heritage Sites across the world. The programme is designed to help preserve sites that are an important part of the world's history. The UNESCO website discusses how World Heritage Sites are selected.

Let's do it!

1. Why do you think Ceren was added to the list of World Heritage Sites in 1993?

2. In what ways is Ceren similar to, and different from, any Maya cities you have already looked at?

3. How similar is Ceren to the modern-day Maya village you looked at in Unit 2.2?

4. Research any UNESCO World Heritage Sites in your country or near where you live. When were they added to the UNESCO list? Why were they added? Make a presentation to your class comparing your chosen UNESCO site with Ceren.

Key word

UNESCO

A modern artist's view of the city of Tikal

Throughout history, people have moved from the countryside to live and work in towns and cities. Jobs have changed from working in the fields to working in factories and shops. Now, about half of the world's population live in cities. The United Nations estimate that, by 2050, nearly 75 per cent of all people in the world will live in urban areas!

When we think of the Maya, we think of their cities, like Tikal, Chichen Itza or Mayapan. We think of great buildings, like pyramids and palaces. We might think

Did more Maya live in the countryside or in the towns and cities?

Urban society

A society where most people live in towns and cities; where there are rulers and ruled; and where learning, technology and industry are much more important than farming.

Rural society

A society where there are fewer people, who live in small villages or isolated houses; and where the most important economic activities are growing food, raising animals and producing raw materials.

of warriors and craftsmen, fighting to keep a powerful state or building grand structures. We don't usually think of villages and farming communities like Ceren. But what is the real picture? From what you have discovered so far, you should now be in a position to decide for yourself whether we should think of the Maya as an urban society or a rural one.

▲
A procession on the walls of the temple at Bonampak

Think about it!

1. Do you agree with the definitions of urban society and rural society? How might you improve these definitions?

2. Do you live in an urban society or a rural one?

3. Do you think the Maya lived in an urban society or a rural one? Why?

Let's do it!

1. Draw two large overlapping circles on a large piece of paper. Label one of them 'urban' and the other one 'rural'. In each circle, list all the reasons you have discovered so far that explain whether the Maya were an 'urban' or 'rural' society. If a reason might fit in both circles, write it in the area where the circles overlap. If a reason does not fit into these categories, write it outside the circles.

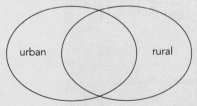

Compare your completed circles to those of others in your group. Are they similar?

2. Which of these conclusions do you agree with?
   a The Maya were an urban society.
   b The Maya were a rural society.
   a The Maya were both urban and rural – one could not exist without the other.

The Spanish, who arrived in what is now Mexico around 1520, both help us and hinder us from understanding the Maya. Bishop Landa arrived in the Yucatán in 1549. His job was to make the Maya into Catholics. He became Archbishop of Yucatán in 1571. He is best remembered for a book he wrote in 1566 which describes much of the Maya religion, beliefs, number system and system of writing. It is from this book that historians in the 19th and 20th centuries began to uncover much of the history of the Maya. However, he also ordered that all Maya books should be burned, and that many of their cities and temples be pulled down. Many of the stones from the temples were reused in Spanish towns and cities in the area, even for building churches and cathedrals!

How did the Maya explain the world they lived in?

One of the ways the Maya explained their world was through science, especially **astronomy**. Many cities had observatories. Some buildings were carefully lined up with the appearance of spring or autumn **equinoxes**, or the appearance of a planet, such as Venus, in the sky. The astronomers could predict **eclipses** of the sun and moon, and their

◀ *A Maya astronomer studies the sky, from the Madrid **codex**. Why do you think the artist has drawn the astronomer's eye the way he has?*

calendar could plot the circuit of Venus around the earth (584 days) to within two hours. And they did all this without a telescope or other optical tools! Predicting eclipses – especially solar eclipses, when day seemed to turn to night – made the astronomers seem very powerful, and helped them to control the people.

Think about it!

1. Why do you think Bishop Landa ordered all Maya books to be burned, and for many temples and palaces to be pulled down?

2. Do you think Bishop Landa's book helps us to understand the Maya, or makes it more difficult to do so?

3. In your opinion, were the Maya good scientists and mathematicians?

Counting

The Maya also developed an inventive way to count. They were one of the first civilisations to use the zero (0), over 1000 years before it was used in Europe. This allowed them to do very complicated calculations, and keep their accounts very accurately. Unlike us, who use a base-10 counting system, the Maya used a base-20 system.

Historians think the Maya used a base-20 system because they used both fingers and toes to count!

The Maya counting system used a series of dots and bars

0	1	2	3	4	5	6	7	8	9

10	11	12	13	14	15	16	17	18	19

Let's do it!

1. Try doing some calculations using the Maya number system. How easy is it to multiply 10 by 5, for example, or divide 100 by 20? Is it easier in Maya numbers, or in the Arabic numerals we are used to?

2. Research a Maya observatory, like the one at Chichen Itza. How did it work? How accurate was it? What part did observatories play in everyday life?

Key words

astronomy

equinoxes

eclipses

codex

The Maya were the only society in Meso-America to develop a written language. They used **hieroglyphs**, or picture writing, like the Ancient Egyptians. So far, historians have discovered over 800 different hieroglyphs! Some pictures show a complete word, like 'cat', whereas others show only one syllable, or part of a word. Some hieroglyphs can be both. Even now, we still cannot decipher every Maya written inscription.

The Maya had over 800 different picture symbols, or hieroglyphs, for writing with!

Hieroglyphs

As we have seen, Bishop Landa ordered all Maya books to be destroyed. Only four are left. These are known as codicies (singular: codex). The picture of the astronomer in Unit 6.1 comes from one of these codices. Despite their being only four codices in existence, there are plenty of other examples of Maya writing for us to study. Murals on the walls of tombs, inscriptions on stelae (see Unit 4.1) and carvings on pyramids and temples all tell us about the Maya.

Maya glyphs from the walls of a temple at the Museo de Sitio in Palenque, Mexico

Measuring the passing of time

The Maya used at least two different calendars. There was one for everyday use, the haab, which was made up of 18 months, each 20 days long, plus a special month of 5 so-called 'unlucky' days. It was much more accurate than any calendar in use in Europe at the time. There was also a 'holy' calendar, the tzolkin, that ran for 260 days, with 20 groups of days each made up of 13 individual days. This was used to set the date of religious festivals. There was also a 'Long Calendar' that covered many centuries.

▲ *A popular representation of the haab calendar*

Think about it!

1. If you had to learn over 800 hieroglyphs, how easy would it be to learn to write? Perhaps it is not surprising that so few Maya could read and write!

2. Why do you think developing a system of writing was so important to the Maya?

Let's do it!

1. Try writing your name in Maya hieroglyphs. How easy is it? (There are lots of websites that can help you.)

2. Find out how the Maya made their books. They didn't use paper. What kind of things did the Maya record in their codices? You could try making your own codex.

3. We have already come across stelae in Unit 4.1. Stelae were erected to praise the achievements of a successful king or ruler. You could design and make your own stela, praising something you have done. What would you include on your stela? To make it more realistic, you could write on your stela in hieroglyphs!

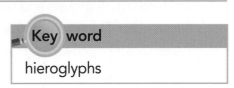

Key word

hieroglyphs

And finally...

Maya gods

The Maya had over 160 different gods, and used the gods to explain their world. Huracan, for example, was the god of wind, and the Maya believed you needed to make sacrifices to him to protect you from hurricanes. Similarly, Chaac was the god of rain – very important in a society dependent on farming. Ix Chel was the goddess of childbirth and medicine. She was always shown as an old woman. Hun Hunahpu was the god of maize and therefore extremely important.

A modern illustration of the goddess of medicine and childbirth, Ix Chel

The maize god was shown in several different forms. In the spring he was shown as a young man; and in the autumn, as without a head, just like the maize that had been recently harvested in the fields.

The Maya maize god, in the British Museum, London

Think about it!

1. Why might the Maya show the maize god in several different forms?
2. Why was it so important for the Maya to keep the gods happy?

Let's do it!

1. Split into small groups and research the Maya gods. Don't forget Kukulkan, who we have already discovered. How do the gods help the Maya to explain their way of life and deal with their problems?
2. Which do you think was more important to the Maya in explaining their world – gods or science? Why?

Writing a focused account and reaching a conclusion

So, just how inventive were the Maya?

At the start of Unit 6.1, we asked the question 'How inventive were the Maya?' We have looked at the ways the Maya viewed the world around them, and how they explained their world. We have explored how they wrote to each other, and how they counted and kept accounts. But only 2–3 per cent of the Maya could read and write, so why were these developments so important? If so few people could read and write, why were a written language and an accurate counting system so important to the Maya? How did it help them live?

Very few Maya could read or write. This made those who could read and write very powerful.

Let's do it!

3. Do you think the Maya were inventive? Make a list of all the factors you have discovered while studying the Maya that suggest they were inventive. Next, make a list of any factors you have discovered that suggest to you that perhaps the Maya were not very inventive. Remember: they were a Stone Age society that had no metal. They built roads but did not have wheeled vehicles, probably because there were no animals that could have pulled them.

   Which list is longer? Which do you think is more convincing? Write a short answer to the question 'How inventive were the Maya?' Think carefully how to structure your answer to make the best possible case.

   Compare your answer to others in your group. Have you all reached the same conclusion? Why are there different opinions about how inventive the Maya were?

Around the year 900 CE, around 90 per cent of the Maya disappeared – or so people used to think. Nowadays, historians are not so sure. It used to be called the Great Collapse. A time when many Maya city-states disappeared completely. Nowadays, it is more likely to be called the Great Descent, when many of the Highland Maya and the Lowland Maya moved to Yucatán.

The Maya region

Think about it!

1. Why do you think there are so many different theories about what happened to the Maya around 900 CE?
2. Which theory do you think is most likely?

Let's do it!

1. Split into groups and research the six theories about the 'collapse' of the Maya. You might find other explanations to add to your list.
2. Feed back to the group. How many different theories do you have altogether?

Key words

abducted   clustered   disrupted

Key ideas why the Maya disappeared around 900 CE

There are all lots of different theories trying to explain events around 900 CE. Some are absurd – for example, the Maya were **abducted** by aliens in a flying saucer! Others are much more realistic. Here are some of the main ideas.

a. **Drought.** There were too many long droughts in the region: from around 820 CE to about 940 CE, and another from around 1000 CE to around 1100 CE. Many cities were abandoned during this time, but not all! The Maya were using too much water, and there was not enough rain.

b. **Warfare.** The Maya were made up of more than 50 city-states, who were often fighting each other. Cities grew when there was a strong king, and shrank when there was a weak ruler. The destroyed city of Yaxchilian, for example, has been excavated. In one small area, over 200 flint spear or arrowheads have been found **clustered** around an entrance to the palace. This is clear evidence of a battle.

c. **Force of nature.** Some historians suggest there was an earthquake or volcanic eruption, like the one that destroyed Ceren in 590 CE (see Unit 5.2). This might have **disrupted** trade and farming and killed thousands of people.

d. **The actions of rulers of the cities**. Some historians say that, at this time, maybe cities were competing to build the biggest, the tallest, the grandest pyramids and temples. This meant thousands of men were building instead of farming, and therefore not enough food was grown.

e. **Climate change brought on by deforestation**. Some historians argue that Maya cities had become too big. By chopping down so many trees for farmland and using so much water, the Maya changed the climate, making it hotter and drier.

f. **The Maya were just too successful!** Because the Maya were clever, inventive and good at farming, they became rich. Rich cities grew bigger. Around 900 CE, perhaps there were just too many Maya in the area. One estimate is that there were over 2 million Maya by this time. They simply could not grow enough food to feed everyone, and that led to fighting and the destruction of city-states.

Deforestation after a volcano eruption

The remains of a deserted Maya city

So, what *did* cause such a collapse? One of the key skills in history is to consider cause and **consequence**. Historians use it a lot to help them understand not just *what* happened, but *why* it happened and then what happened *as a result of* these causes.

Look carefully again at historians' suggestions as to what happened to the Maya (see Unit 7.1 and your own research). Sort the information you have into two columns – 'Cause' and Consequence'. You might use a table like this:

History is complicated – there might be several reasons for the decline in the Maya population.

Cause	Consequence

Causation

Look carefully at your list of 'Causes'. How could you classify them? Perhaps you could use ideas like *short term* (a volcanic eruption, for example) or *long term* (perhaps a drought covering around about 100 years). Does that make it any easier to explain what happened to the Maya?

So far we have only thought in terms of *one* cause. What if two or more causes combined to destroy the Maya way of life? Perhaps a long drought made it more difficult to grow food. Therefore, cities fought each other for land and scarce water resources so they could protect their own city and people? History can be very complicated!

Consequence

Now look at the 'Consequence' column of your table. What were the effects of the events you have been looking at? Was it just that many people died? Which do you think was the most important consequence of these events? Why? Does everyone in your group agree with you?

Interpretations

Historians study events and causes to try to explain what happened in the past. They use the evidence to construct an argument that says what they think happened. In effect, each of the six theories in Unit 7.1 is an **interpretation** of what happened.

Key words
consequence   interpretation

Think about it!

1. To support each of these interpretations, where might you find the evidence you need?
2. What evidence would you need?
3. How would you prove there was a drought at that time? Or that a volcano erupted at just the right moment to cause the end of many Maya cities? We do know that Ceren (Unit 5.2) was destroyed by the eruption of a volcano in about 590 CE.

Let's do it!

1. You should now be in a position to decide what *you* think happened to the Maya around about 900 CE. Think carefully: what evidence do you have to support the reasons you believe to be the best argument?
2. Write your own interpretation of what happened to the Maya. Base it on all the work you have done in Unit 7 so far, but also on the rest of your work on the Maya. Remember: make your argument convincing, and support it with strong evidence.

Modern-day archaeologists at work

The short answer is that nobody knows for sure! That's why it is such a mystery. As you read at the beginning of Unit 7, historians used to think that 90 per cent of all Maya died out around 900 CE. But it is hard to believe that a society that had existed 3000 years (from about 2000 BCE) and built such powerful city-states could just disappear. Historians now think many people survived, and moved to the Yucatán (see map in Unit 7.1) to start a new life. However, cities in Yucatán were nowhere near as big as those in the Southern Uplands. Also, as we know, there are still around 7 million Maya living today in the region.

Drought

Many archaeologists and historians are now convinced that drought was an important part of the answer. Recent research shows there were actually two 'dry' periods around this time. It says that the northern cities in Yucatán that were spared the worst of the 9th-century drought suffered just as badly from the second drought, in the 11th century. Remember: the Maya in the Yucatán depended on underground water supplies called *cenotes,* to irrigate their land and feed people in the cities.

Volcanoes

A volcano might have destroyed Ceren, but some new evidence suggests that volcanic eruptions actually helped the Maya, rather than destroyed them. Volcanic ash is high in nutrients, and layers of ash blowing in the wind following an eruption would make fields many kilometres away more fertile. This would allow more food to be grown and cities to become richer.

▲ *Deforestation today in Meso-America*

A lesson for today

Some historians believe the Maya caused their own downfall to a certain extent. They were just too successful for their own good! By chopping down so many trees, and using up so much water, the Maya altered the climate in Meso-America. They made it hotter and drier, which meant there was not enough food to feed everyone. If that was the case, it is not surprising that **environmentalists** say we should be careful not to follow the example of the Maya.

Did the Maya cause their own downfall?

Think about it!

1. Why do some people use what happened to the Maya as a warning for the way we live in the 21st century?
2. Why can't we decide exactly what happened to the Maya around 900 CE?
3. Do you think we will ever know exactly what happened to the Maya?

Let's do it!

1. Find out what is happening to the rainforest in Meso-America today.
2. Is it fair to suggest we can learn lessons from the actions of the Maya, more than 1000 years ago?

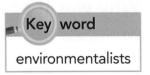

Key word

environmentalists

'In fourteen hundred and ninety-two,
Columbus sailed the ocean blue.'

Christopher Columbus set off from Spain
to sail to the East Indies, in search of
spices he could trade. Instead, he reached
America, and that is why the islands of
the Caribbean are called the West Indies!
It was on his third voyage, in 1502, that
Columbus first came across the Maya.
He met a canoe in his words, 'as large as a
galleon', which contained 24 rowers, 16 passengers and
several bales of cloth to trade along the coast. It didn't take
long for more Spanish explorers to arrive in the region,
searching for treasure.

A painting of Columbus' ship

The Spanish came to
America looking for gold.

Disease

In 1517, a major expedition arrived from Spain to conquer
the Maya. Unfortunately, the Spanish also brought European
diseases like smallpox and measles with them. The Native
Americans had never encountered these illnesses before,
which meant that they had no resistance to them. Some historians estimate that one third
of all Maya died from these European diseases between 1521 and 1523 (in two years!).

Conquest

The Spanish took advantage of the fact that the Maya weren't united in one empire, so
they either sided with one city against another or defeated them one at a time. By 1542,
most cities were defeated, although many Maya fled to the rainforests and continued
to fight a **guerrilla**-style war against the Spanish. It took at least 170 years before the
Spanish managed to totally defeat the Maya.

Why was it so easy for the Spanish to defeat the Maya?

When Maya fought Maya, not many warriors were killed. The battle was about capturing
the leaders of a city and taking them prisoner. The object wasn't to kill, but for one city

to take control of another. Weapons, spears and obsidian axes and knives were relatively simple and used very close up. The Spanish were different. Guns, horses, cannon, crossbows bows and armour all led to a kind of warfare the Maya knew nothing about. Battles were very one-sided, but the Spanish suffered too. Malaria and dysentery killed as many Spanish soldiers as the fighting did.

The Spanish wanted the Maya as slaves. They stole all the best land for themselves. Everything was designed to make Spain rich and the Maya poor.

A modern drawing of a Spanish soldier

Think about it!

1. Imagine you are one of those Maya in the canoe in 1502, and you meet Columbus and his ship. What would you think? How would you feel? What would you say? What would you tell your friends when you got home?

Let's do it!

1. Research the Spanish invasion of the Maya lands. What did the Spanish *expect* to find? What *did* they find? What impact did the Spanish have on the Maya?

2. Look carefully at the images of a Maya warrior (in Unit 4.2) and a Spanish soldier (above). How similar are they, and how different? Which one would you expect to win in a fight? Why?

Key word

guerrilla

47

The West Indies, showing Panama, Santo Domingo and the site of the shipwrecked sailors coming ashore

Shipwreck

In 1511, Gonzalo Guerrero was one of 16 Spanish soldiers and sailors on a ship sailing from Panama to Santo Domingo (capital city of today's Dominican Republic). While at sea, they ran into a severe storm, and their boat was shipwrecked. They managed to climb into a small lifeboat, which lost its sail and oars in the storm. Therefore, they were left to drift helplessly across the sea, but they were finally washed ashore, more dead than alive, on the Yucatán coast. They were captured by the Maya and taken back to a Maya village. Here, they were kept in wooden cages and made to work as slaves in the fields. Some were sacrificed. By 1519, only two – Gonzalo Guerrero and a priest called Geronimo de Aguilar – were still alive. When a man called Hernán Cortés began his invasion of Mexico in 1519, he persuaded Aguilar to join him and act as an interpreter. Gonzalo Guerrero refused to join the Spanish.

> Gonzalo Guerrero was a Spanish sailor who was shipwrecked and kept as a slave by the Maya.

By 1519, Gonzalo was no longer a slave. He was a respected member of the Maya. His skills as a soldier had helped the Maya defend themselves effectively and live peacefully. He had helped build a defensive wall around his town. He had married the daughter of a local chief, and had three children – possibly the first '**mixed race**' children in America. He led the Maya in war. Cortés asked him to choose between his Spanish origins and his Maya life.

Gonzalo successfully led the Maya fight against the Spanish until 1536. This is when he was killed in battle, supporting a neighbouring group of Maya against the Spanish. He was shot by an **arquebus** and died instantly. His Maya warriors collected his body and buried him at sea. This is because he originally came to the Maya from the sea.

◀ *A modern-day statue erected in Yucatán in honour of Gonzalo Guerrero*

Think about it!

1. What would the Maya think about Gonzalo Guerrero?
2. What would the Spanish think about Gonzalo Guerrero?
3. Why do you think a modern statue of Gonzalo Guerrero has been erected in Yucatán?

Let's do it!

1. Why do you think Gonzalo Guerrero decided to stay with the Maya and go against the Spanish? Was he right to do so?
2. Why do you think the heading to this unit is called 'History is complicated!'? How does the story of Gonzalo Guerrero show this?

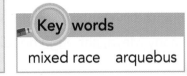

Key words

mixed race   arquebus

There are lots of ancient civilisations in Meso-America we could study – the Olmecs, the Aztecs and, of course, the Incas of South America. There are many other societies throughout history we could study as well. So why study the Maya?

They were successful

From their beginnings around 2000 BCE, the Maya developed a very successful culture. They built cities, pyramids and temples. They were the only Meso-American society to develop a system of writing, some of which scholars still cannot read! They traded throughout the region. They were clever enough to be able to predict eclipses of the sun and moon, and to align buildings with the equinoxes. And they managed to achieve all this without metal or the wheel. We must not forget that the Maya were a Stone Age people.

Some Maya cities had populations of 50,000 or more!

They give us a warning from history

Suddenly, for reasons historians still can't agree on, the Maya went into decline. Cities were deserted and left to become ruins in the jungle. It may have been man-made, through too much deforestation, too much farming and overuse of water. It may have been natural, through drought or volcanic eruption. No one is sure, but maybe it should make us consider what we are doing to our world today.

They still survive today

More than 7 million Maya still live in the region today. This is despite the Spanish conquest, having their cities and culture destroyed and being the poorest citizens in the new countries created in Central America in the 19th century. Many Maya, although not all of them, still live

Rigoberta Menchu, Maya leader and winner of the Nobel Peace Prize

in a traditional way, growing food, making clothes and handicrafts in the way the Maya always have. Despite being Catholics, many still carry on with traditional beliefs and give offerings to their gods. Rigoberta Menchu is a Maya leader who was awarded the Nobel Peace Prize in 1992. She said: 'We are not myths of the past, ruins in the jungle, or zoos. We are people and we want to be respected, not to be victims of **intolerance** and **racism.'** Perhaps the Maya are just as important today as they were in 900 CE.

Think about it!

1. What, in your opinion, was the greatest achievement of the Maya?
2. Why should we remember the Maya today?

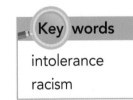

Key words

intolerance

racism

Skills grid

Unit	Skills
1	chronology, sense of period
2	continuity and change
3	significance
4	use of evidence, interpretations
5	similarity and difference, reaching a conclusion
6	writing a focused account, presenting a conclusion
7	cause and consequence, interpretations
8	using historical knowledge to reach a conclusion

Studying the Maya gives you a perfect opportunity to develop some of the skills from the Geography curriculum.

Political geography

It is good to know the location and importance of many of the countries of the world. Studying the Maya gives a perfect opportunity for atlas work, looking at the countries and capital cities of the region. Which is the biggest city? How does it compare in size to the biggest Maya city, Chichen Itza (around 50,000 inhabitants)? And are the Americas one **continent** or two?

Climate study

The Maya lived in **tropical** rainforest. Do you know what a rainforest is? What does 'tropical' mean? How wet is the rainforest? How tall is the **tree canopy**? Which animals live in the rainforest? Are they endangered? Why are there 'wet' and 'dry' seasons? And how does this impact on the area? Are all parts of Central America the same? Is the climate on the Pacific coast the same as on the Caribbean coast? Answering these questions will make it easier to understand the Maya.

We can't understand the lives of the Maya without knowing about the geography of the area.

Map of the Americas

Much of the Maya land is mountainous – the Southern Uplands, for example. How does **altitude** affect temperature and vegetation? Have you ever walked up a mountain? Can you describe some of the effects from personal experience?

How would altitude affect life for the Maya?

Physical geography

Volcanoes played a significant part in the lives of the Maya – either as sources of obsidian for blades and weapons, or as a source of volcanic ash, to fertilise their fields.

The highest volcanoes are in Guatemala. Explore these. Some of them even have webcams!

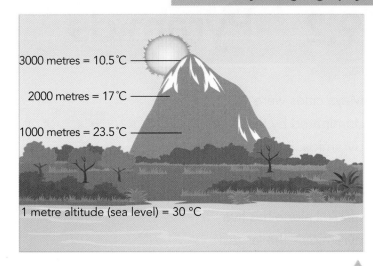

3000 metres = 10.5 °C

2000 metres = 17 °C

1000 metres = 23.5 °C

1 metre altitude (sea level) = 30 °C

How altitude affects climate

The Yucatán Peninsula, where many Maya lived after 900 CE, is a huge limestone **plateau**. Geographers call this a karst landscape. Around 12 per cent of the earth is made up of karst, with examples in every continent. Limestone erodes into fantastic shapes, but is perhaps best known for its underground rivers and caverns. These were used by the Maya as reservoirs and for water storage. Explore how they are formed, and how people use them today.

Deforestation and climate change

We have already seen that many historians think the Maya civilisation declined because of climate change or deforestation (or a combination of both). These issues are talked about today as a major threat to our continued existence. Deforestation – turning land into ranches to raise cattle or into plantations to grow commercial crops – is a major issue throughout the world. This is especially the case in Central and Southern America.

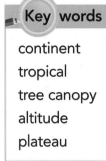

Key words

continent
tropical
tree canopy
altitude
plateau

Think about it!

1. How does studying these aspects of the Geography curriculum make it easier for us to understand life for the Maya long ago?

Let's do it!

1. Learn the names and capital cities of all the countries of the Americas.
2. Which do you think is the most important city in the Americas? Why?
3. In your view, what were the typical features of tropical rainforest?
4. Are volcanoes a threat to humans?
5. Are we responsible for climate change?

Maya cities were dominated by their pyramids. Experts estimate there are over 500 of them. The city of Tikal alone has five pyramids – the largest is over 65 metres tall. Maya pyramids were built as temples to worship the gods, with

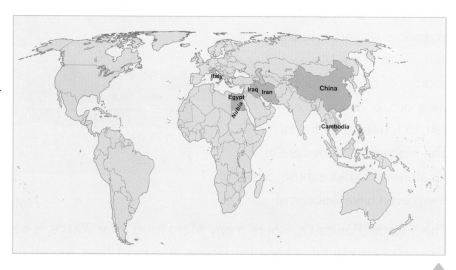

Map showing the countries where there are pyramids

sacrifices taking place on the summit. There is evidence that many pyramids were built over and over on the base of earlier ones. Confusingly, some Maya pyramids were also used as **tombs**!

Ancient Egypt

We think of Egypt as the home of the pyramid. Over 130 have been discovered. They were built from around 2600 BCE to around 1800 BCE. Perhaps the most famous is the Great Pyramid of Giza. It contains at least 2 million stone blocks and stands 137 metres tall. It was built as a tomb for Khufu.

Think about it!

1. Are the pyramids of the Maya and the Ancient Egyptians similar? How do they differ?

More pyramids

There are other pyramids around the world, too. Nubia, now part of the Sudan, has many more pyramids than Egypt, although they are often not as large. There are pyramids in Cambodia (the Prasat Prang temple, for example).

The Great Pyramid at Giza ▶

There are pyramids in Iran and Iraq, known as ziggurats. The most famous is the ziggurat of Ur, which dates from around 2100 BCE and was a temple to the moon goddess, the patron of the city. There are pyramids in China. The **mausoleum** of the first Qin emperor dates from around 250 BCE and has a huge step pyramid at the top. This was originally 76 metres tall and the emperor employed 700,000 men to build it. There is even a pyramid in Rome, built as a tomb for Gaius Cestius in around 18 BCE. Rome had recently conquered Egypt and it is assumed Cestius copied the Egyptian pyramids. However, his is only 37 metres high! It still exists today, and is sometimes open to the public. The pyramid is made of concrete with a curtain of brick, and its exterior is covered with marble.

Cestius' pyramid in Rome

Building pyramids

How did all these societies build such huge pyramids? We know, for example, that the Maya had no animals or wheeled carts, yet managed to drag blocks of stone huge distances. The Egyptians used farm labour during the flood season, when agricultural work was impossible. And how did a Chinese emperor manage to collect 700,000 men to build his tomb?

What were they used for?

We know that the Maya pyramids were mostly built as temples for religious ceremonies, and sometimes had observatories on the top. Egyptian pyramids were tombs for pharaohs – although not all pharaohs were buried in tombs. Were pyramids in other countries also used as temples and burial chambers for rich and powerful rulers?

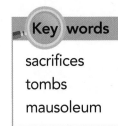

Key words

sacrifices
tombs
mausoleum

Let's do it!

1. Research all the pyramids mentioned above. Make a timeline to show when they were built. Were they all built at the same time, or were some much later than others?

2. From your research, can you tell how they were built? Were all pyramids built in the same way?

3. Which is your favourite pyramid? Why?

The Maya were a Stone Age society. They had no metal tools of any sort. However, they created a very advanced civilisation and managed to farm extensively, build huge cities and develop a complex society.

> *Stone Age societies are usually part of 'prehistory' because there was no writing. But the Maya could write!*

Prehistory

The Stone Age is usually called **prehistory** or 'before history', because there are no written sources. It covers millions of years. At the moment, most historians believe that the first stone tools appeared in what is now Kenya about 2.5 million years ago; the first farmers appeared about 9500 years ago; and bronze started to replace stone at the end of the Stone Age in about 6000 BCE in Africa.

The Stone Age in Britain

▲ *Reconstructed Neolithic houses at Stonehenge*

▲ *Stonehenge*

Think about it!

1. Look carefully at the two images of Stone Age Britain. How similar, and how different, are houses and temples in Britain and in the Maya lands?

2. Where would you have rather lived – Stone Age Britain or in a Maya city? Why?

Stone Age societies today

People think there are around 100 small tribes living today around the world as if they are in the Stone Age. For example, about 200 people live on North Sentinel Island, which is part of the Andaman Islands in the Indian Ocean. They live as **hunter-gatherers**, hunting, fishing and collecting wild plants, and are totally cut off from the rest of the world. There are also some

▲ *A San camp today, in South Africa*

tribes deep in the Amazon rainforest, and in Papua New Guinea, who still live mainly Stone Age lives. However, they come into contact with more and more modern ideas and gadgets over time. There are still a few Australian Aborigines, and the San peoples of the Kalahari Desert in Africa, who cling on to their traditional lifestyle. Perhaps most surprising of all is the Hadzi tribe in Tanzania, a tribe of hunter-gatherers living in the Great African Rift Valley. This is where most historians think life began all those years ago. Most of these tribes live by hunter-gathering, although some do grow some of their own food.

Let's do it!

1. Research one of the Stone Age societies that still exist today. What do they eat? What do they wear? Where do they live? What are their houses like? Their clothes? Their tools and weapons? Report back to the rest of your group.

2. If you could meet one of these people, what five questions would you like to ask them?

3. Do you think their way of life is in danger of **extinction**? If they were to become extinct, what would be lost?

Pulling it all together

You should now be familiar with several different Stone Age societies – the Maya, Stone Age Britain, and a Stone Age society living today. Draw up a list of all the things they have in common, to see how similar they are. What do you notice? Use your list to outline the **characteristics** of a Stone Age people. What would you say to someone who told you that Stone Age people were not very clever?

Key words

prehistory
hunter-gatherers
extinction
characteristics

Glossary

Abducted: stolen

Alabaster: soft white rock used for carving

Altitude: height above sea level

Archaeologists: people who dig up remains and evidence

Arquebus: early form of musket or rifle

Artefacts: objects made by the Maya and left behind as evidence

Astronomy: the study of the sun, moon, stars and planets

Barter: swap, exchange

Beacon: light to guide the way at night

Brash: thin bits of wood left over when trees are chopped down

Canoes: small boats

Canopy: top of the trees

Catastrophe: really bad event

Ceramic: special kind of pottery

Characteristics: special features

City-states: independent countries based on one city and the area immediately around it

Civilisation: complex urban society

Clustered: grouped very, very close together

Codex: Maya book

Consequence: result of

Continent: very large area of land, one big mass but many countries

Contradictory: saying different things

Criteria: things on which something is judged

Disrupted: seriously interrupted

Eclipses: when the light of the sun is obscured by the moon, and vice versa

Environmentalists: people who study the natural world and its problems

Equinoxes: 'equal nights' – the two days a year, in March and September – when both day and night are exactly 12 hours long

Explorers: people who try to discover lost or unknown lands

Extinction: dying out forever

Guerrilla: fighting in small groups, avoiding major battles with a stronger enemy

Hieroglyphs: symbols used as picture writing

Hunter-gatherers: people who move around following animals and collecting fruit

Interpretation: one person's version supported by evidence

Intolerance: refusing to accept views or way of life that is different to your own

Mausoleum: special building housing tomb or tombs

Meso-American: Middle American – the countries we know today as Central America

Mixed race: European and Native American parents

Nutrients: goodness in the soil that helps crops grow

Observatories: special places for studying the sky

Obsession: totally preoccupied by it

Phoenicians: ancient civilisation based around Lebanon; very successful trading nation around 1500 BCE

Plantations: very large farms

Plateau: area of fairly level high ground

Prehistory: time before history; before written records

Racism: discriminating against someone because of their race, thinking your own race is superior

Resilient: recover quickly from a bad event

Sacrifices: special offerings to a god or gods

Seasonal: just for part of the year

'Slash And burn': cut down trees and burn them to clear forests for farming

Tombs: graves, burial places

Tree canopy: highest trees in the rain forest

Tribute: special tax or gift

Tropical: between the Tropic of Cancer and the Tropic of Capricorn, around the equator

UNESCO: The United Nations Educational, Scientific and Cultural Organization, in Paris

Index

World map

North Pole

GREENLAND

ICELAND   NORWAY   SWE

CANADA

UNITED
KINGDOM DENMAR

IRELAND

GERMAN

AUST

FRANCE   CRO

UNITED STATES
OF AMERICA

PORTUGAL   SPAIN   ITAI

MOROCCO

MEXICO

ALGERIA   L

CUBA

MAURITANIA   MALI

NIGER

JAMAICA

SENEGAL

GUATEMALA

NICARAGUA

GUINEA

NIGERIA

COSTA RICA

VENEZUELA

GHANA

PANAMA

GUYANA

COLOMBIA

ATLANTIC
OCEAN

Equator

ECUADOR

GABON

PERU

BRAZIL

PACIFIC
OCEAN

BOLIVIA

NAM

PARAGUAY

CHILE

URUGUAY

ARGENTINA

SOUTHERN O

South Pole

ARCTIC OCEAN

RUSSIA

KAZAKHSTAN

MONGOLIA

JAPAN

PACIFIC
OCEAN

INE

TURKEY

TURKMENISTAN

SYRIA

RAEL

IRAQ

JORDAN

IRAN

AFGHANISTAN

CHINA

YPT

SAUDI
ARABIA

PAKISTAN

NEPAL

OMAN

INDIA

MYANMAR

JDAN

ERITREA YEMEN

THAILAND

PHILIPPINES

VIETNAM

OUTH
UDAN

ETHIOPIA

SOMALIA

SRI
LANKA

MALAYSIA

Equator

KENYA

IC
OF
O

INDIAN
OCEAN

INDONESIA

PAPUA NEW
GUINEA

TANZANIA

SOLOMON
ISLANDS

IA

MOZAMBIQUE

VANUATU

MADAGASCAR

AUSTRALIA

NEW
ZEALAND

Acknowledgements

The publishers wish to thank the following for permission to reproduce images. Every effort has been made to trace copyright holders and to obtain their permission for the use of copyright materials. The publishers will gladly receive any information enabling them to rectify any error or omission at the first opportunity.

(t = top, c = centre, b = bottom, r = right, l = left)

p4b Wollertz/Shutterstock; p5 Pyramidal building and Fragments of Sculpture at Copan, from 'Views of Ancient Monuments in Central America, Chiapas and Yucatan', 1844 (colour litho), Catherwood, Frederick (1799-1854)/ Private Collection/Bridgeman Images; p6b and 9t Roberto Fumagalli/Alamy Stock Photo; p7 VICTOR TORRES/ Shutterstock; p8b Aztravels/Shutterstock; p10 bumihills/Shutterstock; p11 Peek Creative Collective/Shutterstock; p12t RaksyBH/Shutterstock; p12b mauritius images GmbH/Alamy Stock Photo; p13 Lena Wurm/Shutterstock; p17 Gustavo Frazao/Shutterstock; p18 nnattalli/Shutterstock; p19 mauritius images GmbH/Alamy Stock Photo; p20 Ondrej Prosicky/Shutterstock; p22 Lukiyanova Natalia frenta/Shutterstock; p23 Diego Grandi/Shutterstock; p25 Leon Rafael/ Shutterstock; p26 Rebius/Shutterstock; p27 Joraca/Shutterstock; p30 Matyas Rehak/Shutterstock; p31l Daniel Andis/ Shutterstock; p31r Dennis Cox/Alamy Stock Photo; p32 Public domain; p33t robertharding/Alamy Stock Photo; p34 World History Archive/Alamy Stock Photo; p36 Ariadne Van Zandbergen/Alamy Stock Photo; p37 Panther Media GmbH/Alamy Stock Photo; p38t Julio Aldana/Shutterstock; p38b Stefano Ravera/Alamy Stock Photo; p42l Juliet Ferguson/Alamy Stock Photo; p42r AGF Srl/Alamy Stock Photo; p44 Eye Ubiquitous/Alamy Stock Photo; p45 National Geographic Image Collection/Alamy Stock Photo; p46 Niday Picture Library/Alamy Stock Photo; p49 Gonzalo Guerrero, 1974 (bronze), Arellano, Raul Ayala (b.1940) / Akumal, Tulum, Quintana Roo, Mexico / Photo © Ken Welsh / Photo © Ken Welsh / Bridgeman Images; p50 WENN Rights Ltd/Alamy Stock Photo; p51 Ray Waddington/Alamy Stock Photo; p54b Copycat37/Shutterstock; p55 Alvaro German Vilela/Shutterstock; p56l Andrea De la Parra/Shutterstock; p56r Drone Explorer/Shutterstock; p57 2630ben/Shutterstock.